Directions:

Start at the green dot, follow the arrows.

Hop or jump to the number 2, if it is a two-step letter,

and continue to follow the arrows.

These alphabet letter formation poems: use finger tracing to teach

the left to right progression needed for future handwriting success.

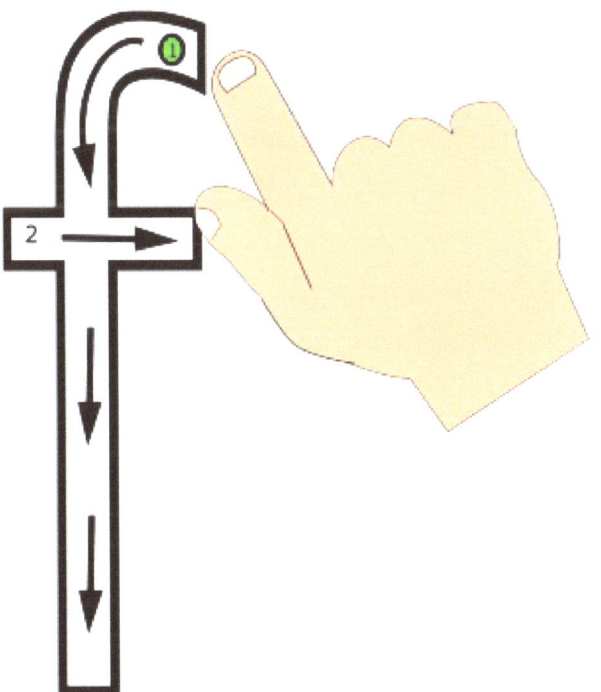

To my wonderful husband: Thank you for all your support & encouragement through the decades. You helped me so much with all my books.

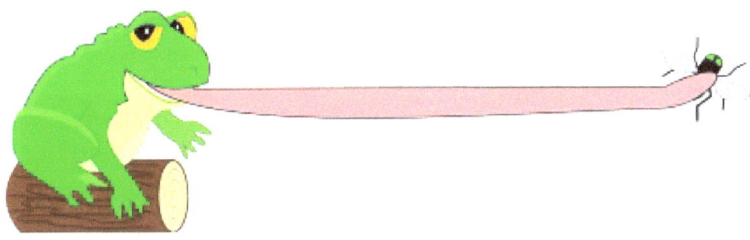

Text and Illustrations copyright © D. Passmore 2019 Pure Joy Teaching

No part of this publication may be reproduced, stored in a retrieval system, or transmitted in any form or by any means, electronic, mechanical, photocopying, recording, or otherwise, without the written permission of the copyright owner. All graphic illustrations are copyrighted.© D. Passmore 2019

ISBN: 978-0-473-47258-0

All graphic illustrations are copyrighted. © D. Passmore 2019
Third Edition 2020

Andy ant marches around the apple, then turns and goes back down to his mound in the ground.

Ben the bear goes straight down from his den! Then turns and walks all the way around the blueberry tree, chased by the buzzing bees.

Casey the caterpillar chews along a cabbage leaf. She enjoys her half circle treat, before a cocoon sleep.

Dizzy dinosaur dances around, then drags his tail up and slams it down to knock all the donuts to the ground.

Eddie eel makes an electric line in the middle! Then swims around in a half circle, to hide in his little cave.

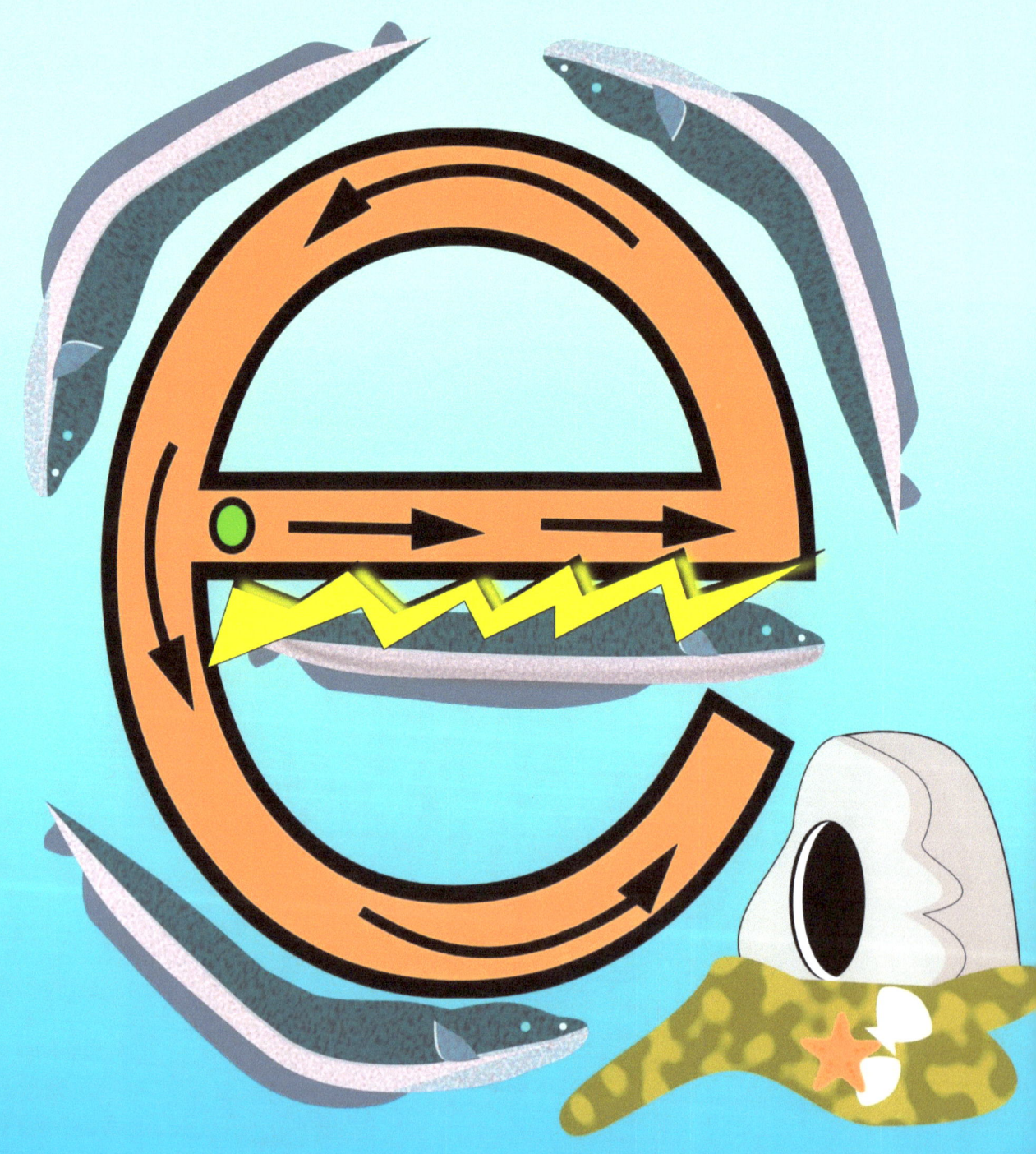

Freddie the frog dives down, then hops up! He snaps his tongue across to the other side to get a juicy fly.

Greg the gopher goes around the golf ball, turns down and makes a goofy hook to grab green grapes.

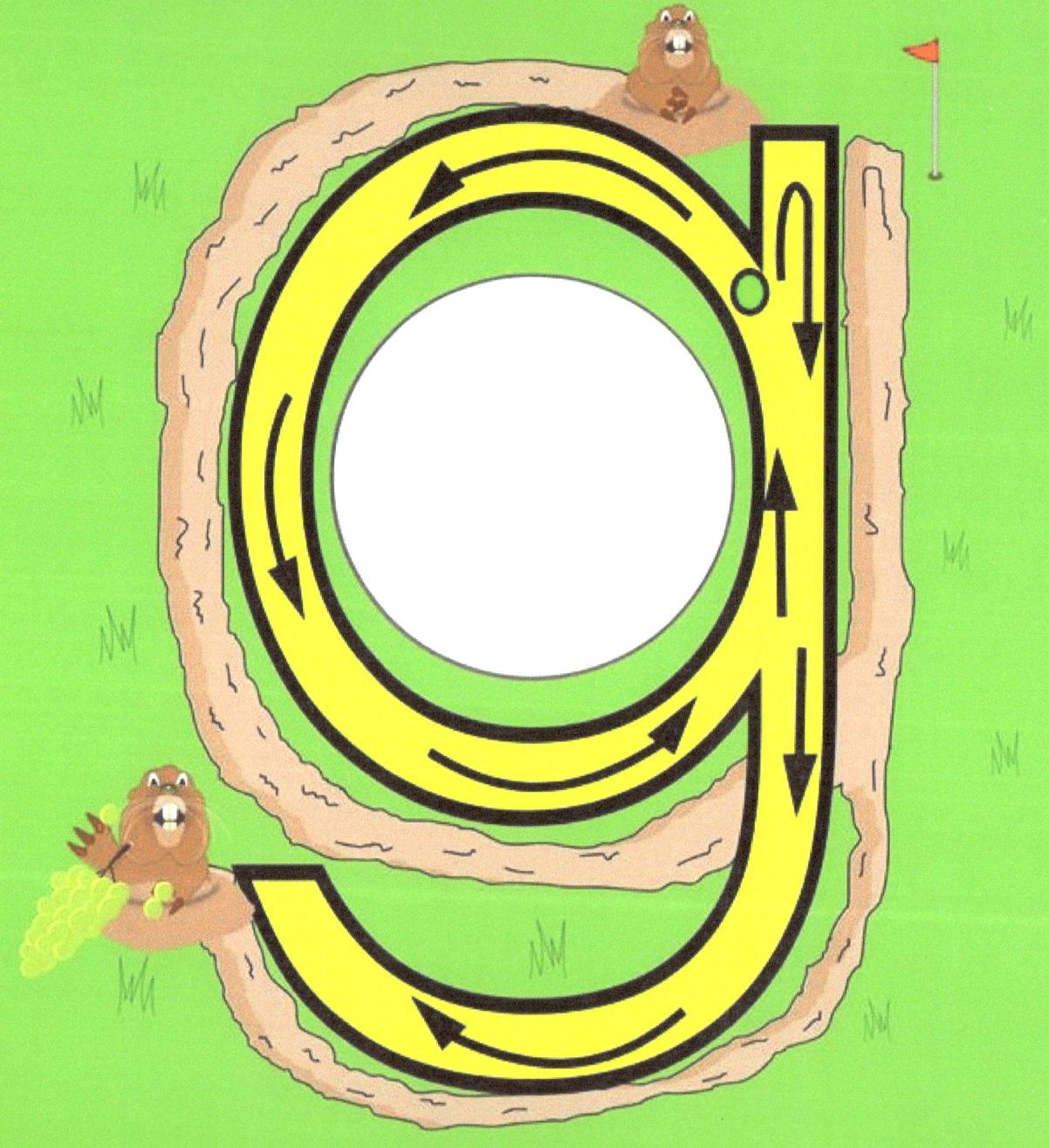

Harry the horse runs straight out the barn, then he hops over the hay and yells hooray!

Icky inchworm lays very flat, put a dot on top, because he blew off his hat.

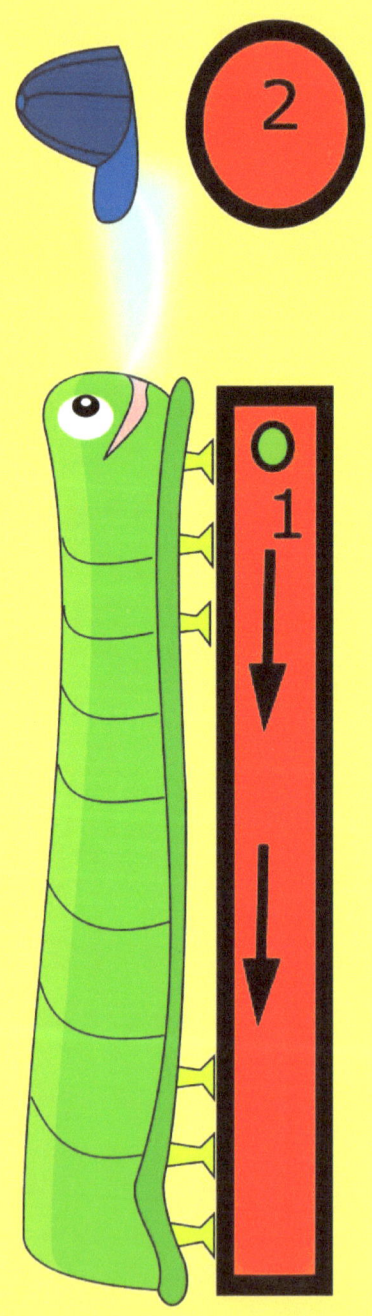

Jenny the jellyfish swings down with a curl,
under the sun that shines more than a pearl.

Kim the koala sits straight in a tree, she pulls on the branches and pushes with her feet.

Long lazy lizard lays on the floor,
he is as straight as a board.

Mike the monkey drops down from the tree! Then bounces over the mountains of mangos and melons and lands in the mush.

Neil the newt lays down flat! Then swipes his tail over to knock noodles into a nest.

Oliver the octopus rolls oysters and oranges around in a circular motion in the ocean.

Peter the puffin plops down into the pool! Then hops up and parades around the polar bear to get some popcorn to share.

Quentin the quail quietly goes around the queen's crown! Then he drags her long quilt down to the ground.

Ricky the rabbit races down to the line!
Then runs up and hops over a rock
to get to the radishes.

Sam the snake slides around and between two sleeping snails to drink a strawberry shake.

Tommy the tiger drops down to tag a turtle! Then hops up to lay on a branch of the tree.

Uncle umbrella bird flies under the underwear, turns up and then goes down.

Vinny the vulture vrooms down and then up, by the light of the moon.

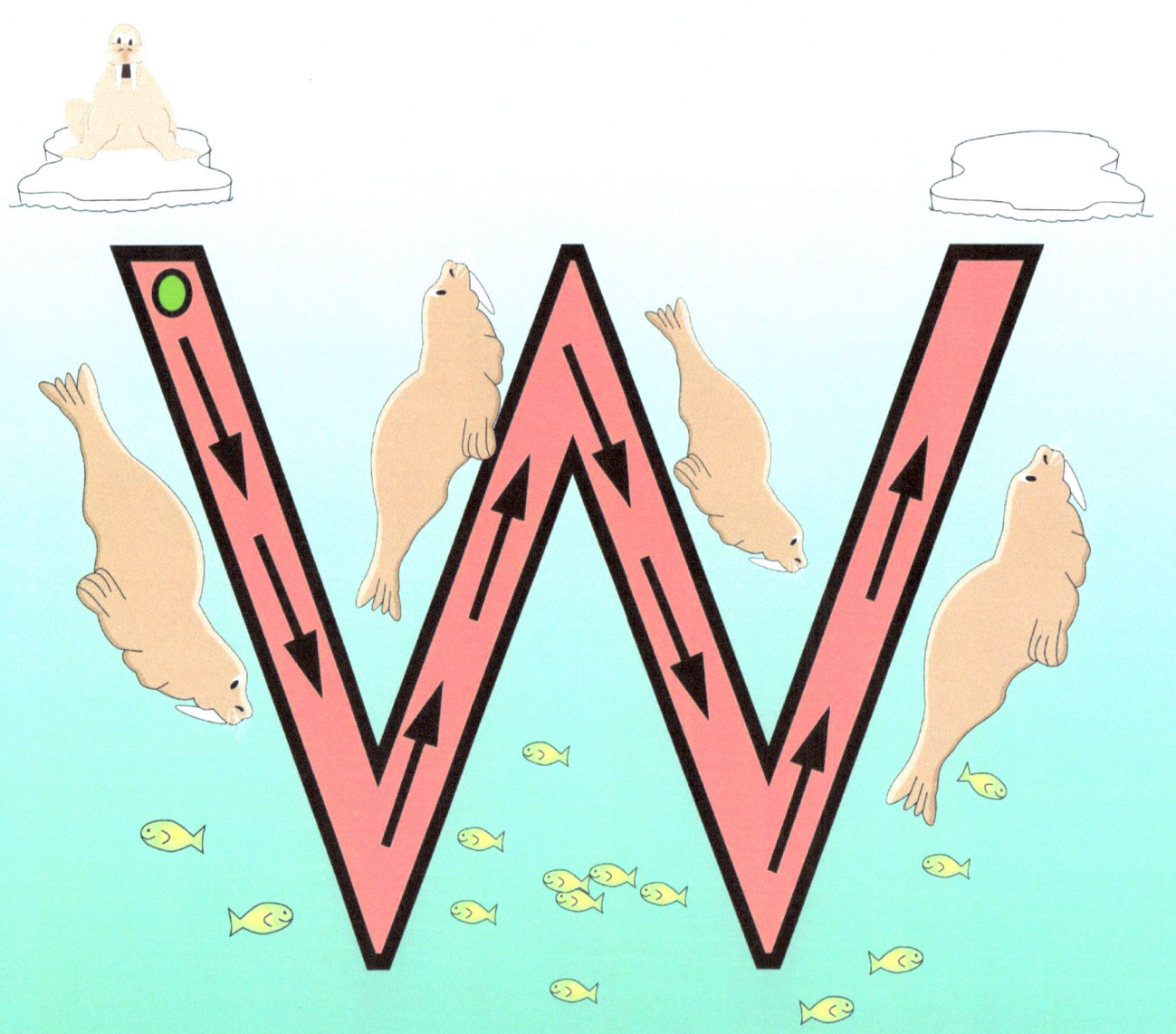

Walter the walrus dives down in the water and comes up! Then dives down and comes up again to get twice as much fish.

One X-ray fish exits at an angle! Then the other crosses from the opposite side to avoid getting into a tangle.

Yancy the yak rolls a yoyo only halfway! The second time he rolls, it goes under the hay.

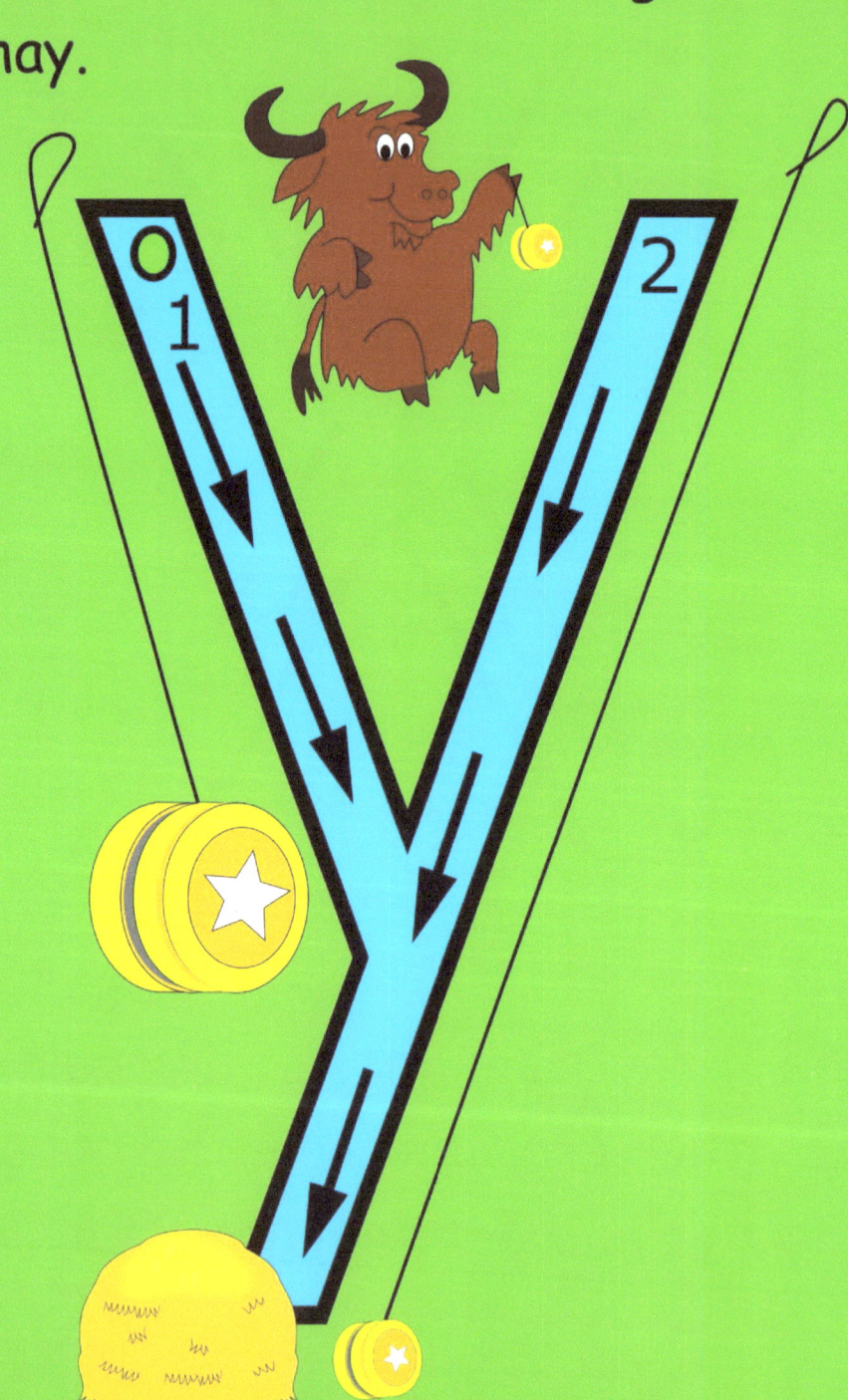

Zack the zebra zips across, then zags down, then zigs back across again to his pen.

I spy

I spy

I spy

I spy

Give instruction to a wise man, and he will be still wiser; Teach a just man, and he will increase in learning.

Proverbs 9:9

Look for more books by D. Passmore

 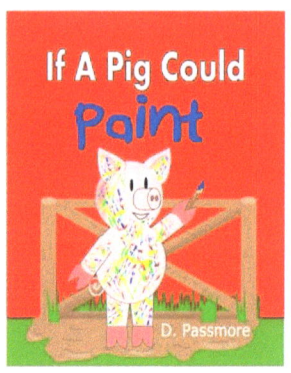 

978-0-473-40992-0   978-0-473-44305-4   978-0-473-43857-9

Find resources for teachers at my shop:

Teachers pay teachers pure-joy-teaching

Download printables for these books and more.

https://www.teacherspayteachers.com/Store/Pure-Joy-Teaching

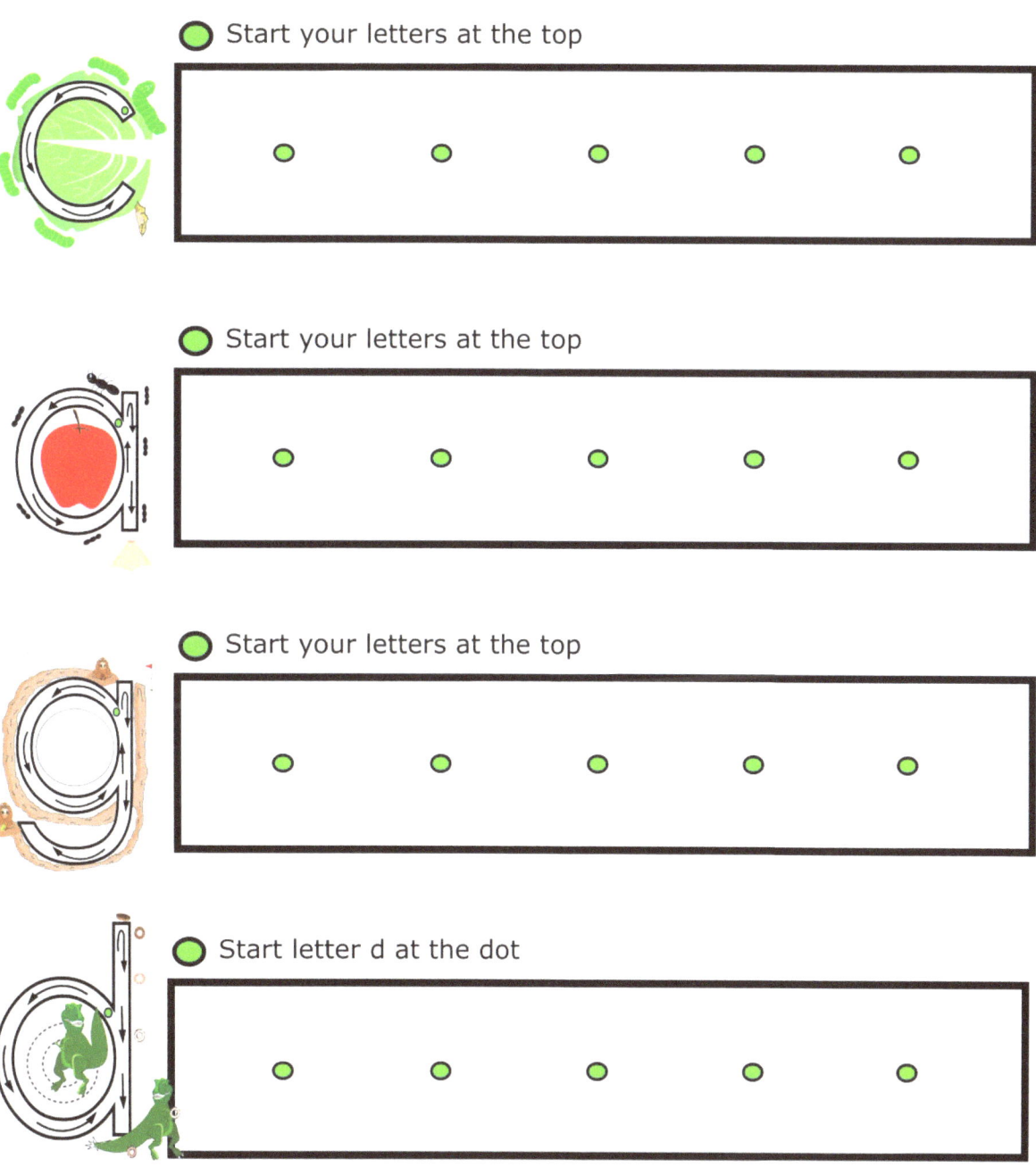

Workbook Sample

All of these letters have the same letter c shape in them. Grouping them together for handwriting practice can help eliminate letter reversal errors.

- Start your letters at the top
- Start your letters at the top
- Start your letters at the top
- Start letter d at the dot

© D.Passmore Pure Joy Teaching   Awesome Animal Alphabet Poems: ABC

www.ingramcontent.com/pod-product-compliance
Lightning Source LLC
LaVergne TN
LVHW072057070426
835508LV00002B/143